# THE CALIFORNIA GOLD RUSH

BY BEATRICE HARRIS

Gareth Stevens
PUBLISHING

CRASHCOURSE

**Please visit our website, www.garethstevens.com. For a free color catalog of all our high-quality books, call toll free 1-800-542-2595 or fax 1-877-542-2596.**

**Library of Congress Cataloging-in-Publication Data**
Names: Harris, Beatrice, author.
Title: The California Gold Rush / Beatrice Harris.
Description: New York : Gareth Stevens Publishing, [2022] | Series: A look
  at U.S. history | Includes bibliographical references and index.
Identifiers: LCCN 2020024426 (print) | LCCN 2020024427 (ebook) | ISBN
  9781538266359 (library binding) | ISBN 9781538266335 (paperback) | ISBN
  9781538266342 (set) | ISBN 9781538266366 (ebook)
Subjects: LCSH: California--Gold discoveries--Juvenile literature. |
  California--History--1846-1850--Juvenile literature.
Classification: LCC F865 .H1767 2022  (print) | LCC F865  (ebook) | DDC
  979.4/04--dc23
LC record available at https://lccn.loc.gov/2020024426
LC ebook record available at https://lccn.loc.gov/2020024427

First Edition

Published in 2022 by
**Gareth Stevens Publishing**
111 East 14th Street, Suite 349
New York, NY 10003

Editor: Therese Shea

Photo credits: Series art Christophe BOISSON/Shutterstock.com; (feather quill) Galushko Sergey/Shutterstock.com; (parchment) mollicart-design/Shutterstock.com; cover, p. 1 Spencer Weiner/Los Angeles Times via Getty Images; p. 5 Stock Montage/Getty Images; pp. 7, 13, 21 Bettmann/Getty Images; pp. 9, 27 GraphicaArtis/Getty Images; p. 11 (top) ullstein bild/ ullstein bild via Getty Images; p. 11 (bottom) G.F. Nesbitt & Co., printer/ NorCalHistory/ Wikipedia.org; p. 15 Fourleaflover/ iStock / Getty Images Plus; p. 17 The Print Collector/Print Collector/Getty Images; p. 19 Hulton Archive/Getty Images; p. 23 Universal History Archive/ Getty Images; p. 25 H. Armstrong Roberts/ClassicStock/Getty Images; p. 29 duncan1890/ DigitalVision Vectors/Getty Images.

Printed in the United States of America

Some of the images in this book illustrate individuals who are models. The depictions do not imply actual situations or events.

CPSIA compliance information: Batch #CSGS22: For further information contact Gareth Stevens, New York, New York at 1-800-542-2595.

Find us on

# CONTENTS

Words in the glossary appear in **bold** type the first time they are used in the text.

# THE RUSH FOR GOLD

The California gold rush was an event that changed the United States in the mid-1800s. When people heard gold was found, they rushed to California. For many, this was a long, hard trip. They hoped to become rich in the new American **territory**.

# GOLD MINERS HEADED TO CALIFORNIA

# MARSHALL'S DISCOVERY

The story of the gold rush begins on January 24, 1848, in Coloma, California. A man named John Sutter was building a **sawmill** next to the American River. One of his workers, James Marshall, found small bits of gold in the river.

SUTTER'S MILL

## MAKE THE GRADE

John Sutter was a businessman who came to
California from Switzerland. He founded a
community that became Sacramento, California.

Sutter and Marshall tried to keep the gold a secret. However, the news spread. People began to arrive by boat to search for gold. At first, they came from places such as Oregon, Mexico, China, and what is now called Hawaii.

SAN FRANCISCO HARBOR, AROUND 1850

# NEWS MOVES EAST

By the end of 1848, the news about California gold had traveled to the East Coast. In 1849, tens of thousands made the long trip to try to get rich. These people, mostly men, came to be called forty-niners.

# BY SEA

There were three ways to reach California from the East Coast. People sailed around Cape Horn at the southern end of South America. They also could sail to Panama. Then, they walked or rode a horse across the **isthmus** and sailed up the West Coast.

13

# BY LAND

The third way to California was across the **continent**. In 1849, more than 25,000 people traveled an overland route to California by wagon or on foot. The California Trail began in Independence, Missouri. The way was over 2,000 miles (3,219 km) long.

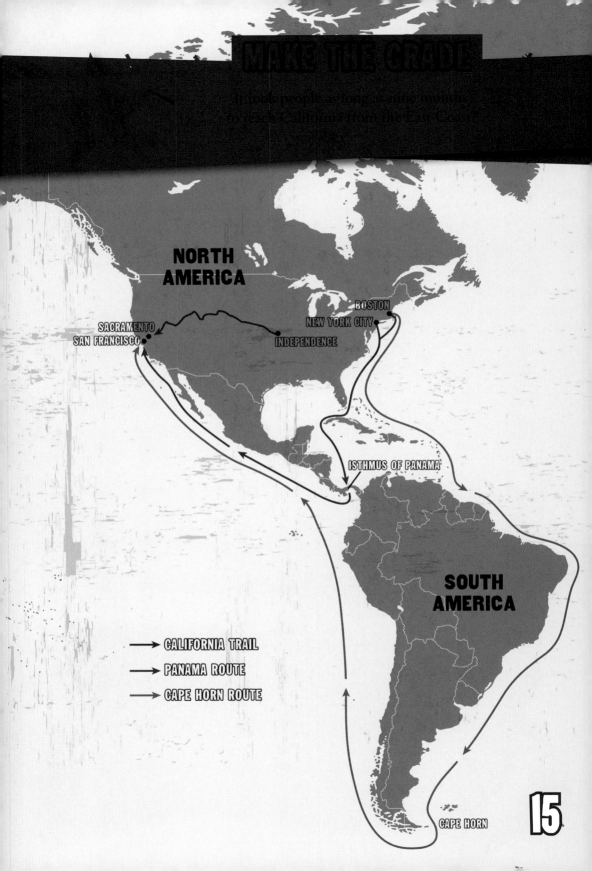

# MAKE THE GRADE

It took people as long as nine months to reach California from the East Coast.

NORTH AMERICA

SOUTH AMERICA

BOSTON

NEW YORK CITY

SACRAMENTO

SAN FRANCISCO

INDEPENDENCE

ISTHMUS OF PANAMA

CAPE HORN

→ CALIFORNIA TRAIL

→ PANAMA ROUTE

→ CAPE HORN ROUTE

15

# HOW TO FIND GOLD

Panning for gold was one way people tried to find it. Rocks and dirt were placed in a pan. Then, miners shook the pan. Because gold is heavy, it dropped to the pan's bottom. Later, larger tools called rockers, or cradles, were used.

# THE LIFE OF A MINER

Gold mining wasn't easy. Gold miners worked in cold rain and hot sun. Some slept in tents, others in poorly built cabins, and many just under trees. Miners were often tired, hungry, dirty, and sick. Many miners died because of the bad conditions.

## MAKE THE GRADE

Both enslaved and free Black Americans came to California to find gold. In 1850, when California became a state, slavery was made illegal there.

19

# THE CHINESE IN CALIFORNIA

Life was even harder for the Chinese people who had come to find gold. They dealt with **racism** and **violence**. They had to pay higher taxes too. Many Chinese moved to California because of hard times in China.

# WHO GOT RICH?

The first people to search for gold had an easier time finding it. Later, most did the hard work and didn't find anything. Many who set up businesses for miners became richer than those looking for gold. They sold clothing, food, and other supplies.

# MAKE THE GRADE

Some business fields appeal to
high prices, they could cost you so much
for making money.

# POPULATION BOOM

In 1846, California's population included about 150,000 Native Americans, 6,500 people of Spanish or Mexican **descent**, and about 700 people from the United States or other places. In 1849, more than 100,000 forty-niners arrived. By 1853, more than 250,000 gold seekers were in California.

## MAKE THE GRADE

After the gold rush
Native American
died from disease

# BOOMTOWNS

As miners moved from place to place looking for gold, towns built up around them. These were called boomtowns. Some were **abandoned** when people couldn't find gold and moved on. A few of these are called ghost towns today. People can still visit them.

# MAKE THE GRADE

San Francisco, California, was a small town when
the gold rush began. It grew very fast. People used
the wood from ships in the port for new buildings.

# THE END OF THE GOLD RUSH

After 1852, less gold was found each year in California. People began to work for **hydraulic** mining companies. These businesses had tools to find gold under the earth. The gold rush in California ended by the late 1850s.

# A TIMELINE OF
## THE CALIFORNIA GOLD RUSH

**1848**

In January, James Marshall finds gold in Coloma, California.

**1849**

Tens of thousands travel to California to mine gold.

**1850**

California becomes the 31st U.S. state.

**1851**

San Francisco's port is crowded with 465 ships.

**1852**

About $81 million of gold is found in the richest year of the gold rush.

**1853**

Hydraulic mining is invented.

**1854**

A Chinese newspaper begins in California.

**1855**

More than 300,000 people have arrived in California since the gold rush began.

**1857**

The amount of gold found is down to $45 million per year.

**1859**

The California gold rush comes to an end.

# GLOSSARY

**abandon:** to leave empty or uncared for

**continent:** one of Earth's seven great landmasses

**descent:** connected to a family or group of people

**disease:** an illness

**enslaved:** being owned by another person and forced to work without pay

**hydraulic:** operated using the pressure of a liquid

**immigrant:** one who comes to a country to settle there

**isthmus:** a narrow strip of land that joins two larger land areas

**population:** the number of people living in an area

**racism:** the belief that people of different races have different qualities and abilities and that some are superior or inferior

**sawmill:** a machine or building in which wood is sawed

**territory:** a part of the United States that isn't a state and has its own government

**violence:** the act of using force to harm someone

# FOR MORE INFORMATION

## Books

Blashfield, Jean F. *The California Gold Rush and the '49ers*. North Mankato, MN: Capstone Press, 2018.

Morlock, Theresa. *The Gold Rush*. New York, NY: Britannica Educational Publishing, 2018.

## Websites

**California Gold Rush**
*www.ducksters.com/history/westward_expansion/california_gold_rush.php*
Read more interesting facts about this important time.

**The California Gold Rush**
*www.pbs.org/wgbh/americanexperience/features/goldrush-california/*
There's more to learn about the gold rush on this site.

**Publisher's note to educators and parents:** Our editors have carefully reviewed these websites to ensure that they are suitable for students. Many websites change frequently, however, and we cannot guarantee that a site's future contents will continue to meet our high standards of quality and educational value. Be advised that students should be closely supervised whenever they access the internet.

# INDEX